Why make terrible detectives?

Because they always melt under pressure!

What do you call a snowman that can play the piano?

A brrr-illiant musician!

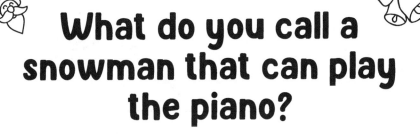

Why did the gingerbread man go to school?

To become one smart cookie!

MW01148975

How does Santa keep his pants up?

With a snow belt!

Why did the tree go to the barber?

It needed a trim!

Why did the Snowman pick a carrot?

He needed a nose!

Why was the tree so popular?

Because everyone was pining for it!

How do snowmen get around?

By riding an icicle!

Why do cats love Christmas?

Because of Sandy Claws!

What's Santa's favorite math?

Adding presents!

Why was the elf sad?

He had low elf-esteem!

Why don't trees sew?

They keep dropping needles!

Why did Santa take music lessons?

He wanted jingle bells!

Why did the Snowman work out?

He had snow abs!

Why was the letter "N" proud?

It starts Noel!

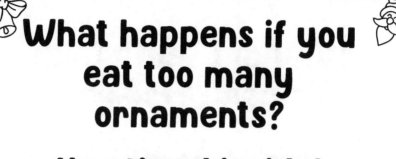

What happens if you eat too many ornaments?

You tinsel inside!

What's Santa's favorite dance?

The Jingle Bell Rock!

Who delivers Christmas presents to cats?

Santa Paws!

Why was the turkey at the Christmas party so proud?

Because it was stuffed!

What did the gingerbread man use to fix his house?

Icing and gumdrop nails, but he had to watch out for sweet-toothed intruders!

Why did Rudolph start attending school?

He wanted to improve his "light-erature" skills!

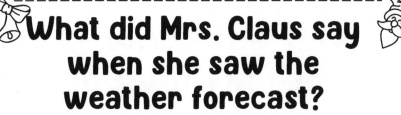

What did Mrs. Claus say when she saw the weather forecast?

"Looks like rein, deer, tonight!"

What do Santa's helpers use when they take notes?

Elf-help books!

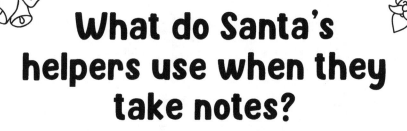

Why did the Snowman want a job in sales?

He heard it was a cool commission!

What's Santa's favorite type of potato?

The North Poutine!

What's the Grinch's favorite board game?

Mean-opoly, but he often has a change of heart!

Why did the Christmas bell get a promotion?

It always rang out the best in everyone!

What did the snowman order at the restaurant?

"Ice'll have the usual!"

Why did the ornament go to school?

Because it wanted to be a little "brighter"!

What's Rudolph's favorite type of music?

Anything with a bright note!

Why did the Christmas candle go to college?

To brighten its prospects!

What did Santa say to Mrs. Claus when he lost his belt?

"I guess it's time to buckle down!"

How do Christmas trees get online?

They log in but always pine for faster internet!

Why did Rudolph get in trouble?

His nose was too bright!

How does Santa know which house to go to?

He checks his list!

Why did the snow lady break up with the Snowman?

Because he had a cold personality!

Why does Santa hate tight spaces?

He's Claus-trophobic!

Why was the Snowman rummaging through a box of crayons?

He wanted to find the best shade of carrot.

Who's the mafia boss at the North Pole?

Al Claus-pone.

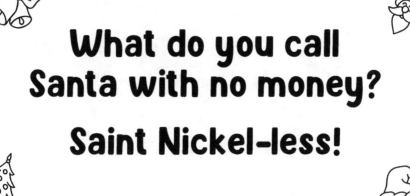

What do you call Santa with no money?

Saint Nickel-less!

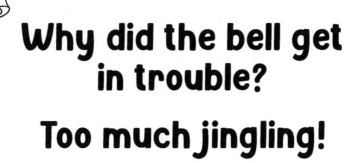

Why did the bell get in trouble?

Too much jingling!

Who gives sharks presents?

Santa Jaws!

How does Christmas end?

With the letter S!

What did the snow say to its friend?

"You melt my heart!"

What's has long sideburns and sings at Christmas?

Elf-is Presley!

Why do mummies love Christmas so much?

Because of all the wrapping!

How did the snow globe feel this year?

A little shaken!

Why did the gingerbread go to the bank?

To get his dough back!

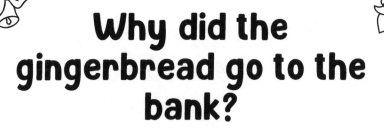

How do you know when Santa's in the room?

You can sense his presents!

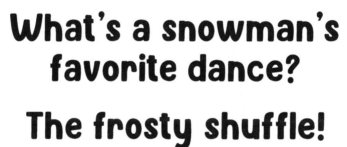

What's a snowman's favorite dance?

The frosty shuffle!

What did the gingerbread man use to fix his house?

Icing and gumdrops!

What's the Snowman's favorite cereal?

Frosted Flakes!

What's a snowman's temper called?

Snow-rage!

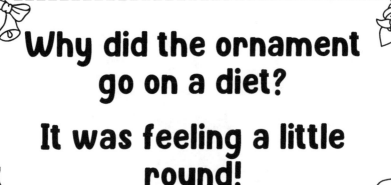

Why did the ornament go on a diet?

It was feeling a little round!

What did the Christmas tree say to the decoration?

"Aren't you tired of hanging around?"

Why did the elf go to school?

To learn his "elf"-abet!

What do you call a reindeer that tells jokes?

A Come-deer!

How did the ornament get a part in the school play?

It was a tree-mendous actor!

What do you call a Santa who walks backward?

Santa Retreat!

Why did the Snowman name his dog "Freeze"?

Because "Freeze" always stayed by his side, even when things got heated!

How does the Snowman stay informed?

He reads the frosty forecast!

Why did the snowgirl dump the snowboy?

She found out he was snow good for her!

Why did the Grinch join a gym?

To bulk up his holiday spirit!

Why did the Snowman apply to an office?

He wanted a warm reception!

What does a snowman wear when he's feeling cold?

An ice-olated jacket!

What do snowmen like to do on the weekend?

Chill out!

How do you know if Santa's been in your garden shed?

You find Claus marks on your tools!

Why did the Snowman apply for a job at the bakery?

He heard they were looking for a roll model!

What do snowmen call their kids?

Chill-dren!

Why did Rudolph get a promotion?

Because he was always "nose-ing" ahead in his work!

Why was the Snowman always calm?

Because he knew how to keep his cool!

What do Santa and his reindeer use when they get hurt?

The first "elf" kit!

What did one ornament say to another?

"I like hanging with you!"

How do you scare a snowman?

Get a hairdryer!

Why did Santa bring a blanket to the beach?

He didn't want to be Sandy Claus!

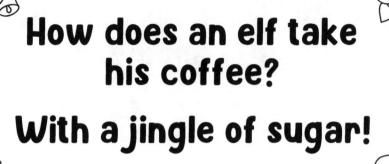

How does an elf take his coffee?

With a jingle of sugar!

Why was the Snowman searching for his checkbook?

He wanted to keep his "ice"-sets liquid!

Who's the most mannerless reindeer?

Rude-dolph!

How does Santa greet children in Hawaii?

"Aloho-ho-ho!"

Why did the ornament go to rehab?

It got hooked on tinsel!

Why did the Snowman turn yellow?

Ask the dog.

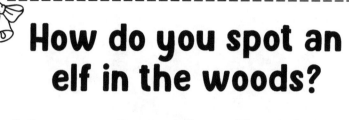

How do you spot an elf in the woods?

Listen for the jingle of bells!

Why was the math worksheet so festive?

It had too many tree-angles!

What did the gingerbread man use to make his bed?

A cookie sheet!

Why did Frosty ask for a calendar for Christmas?

To have 12 months of cool days!

Why did the Snowman go to art school?

Because he wanted to be a "cool" artist!

Why did the elf bring a sketchbook to the party?

To draw some fun!

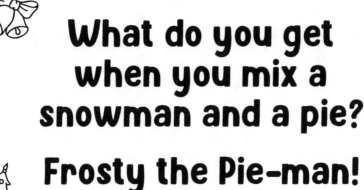

What do you get when you mix a snowman and a pie?

Frosty the Pie-man!

Why did the reindeer wear sunglasses?

Because of the snow glare!

What do you get when you cross Santa with a gardening tool?

"Hoe, hoe, hoe!"

Why did the Snowman bring string to the party?

He wanted to tie one on!

What do you call a Santa who works in a law firm?

Santa "Clause"!

Why did the elf have a notebook?

He had lists to double-check!

How did the Snowman feel when he saw the sun?

Melt-down!

Why was the math book at the top of Santa's naughty list?

Because it had too many problems!

How do you greet an alien at Christmas?

"Merry Christmas to all life forms!"

Why did the Snowman break up with the snow-woman?

He was cold-hearted!

Why did Santa wear a raincoat?

Because of the rein, dear!

How do you know a snowman is in a bad mood?

He gives everyone the cold shoulder!

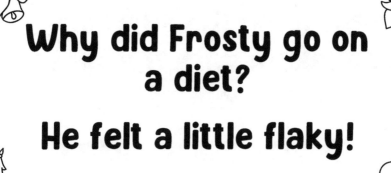

Why did Frosty go on a diet?

He felt a little flaky!

Why did the snowgirl apply lipstick?

To get frosted lips!

What did the gingerbread man use to surf the web?

His crumb-puter!

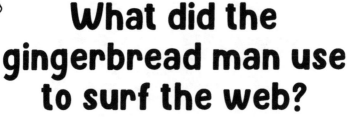

Why did the ornament audition?

It wanted to be a pop star!

Why was the Snowman looking at vegetables?

He wanted to pick a fresh nose!

Why did the Snowman give a ticket?

He was a snow patrol!

What did the big
ornament say to the
small one?

"You're bauble-icious!"

What do you call a T-
Rex dressed as Santa?

Santa Claws!

How did the
Snowman get his job?

He was ice to everyone
during the interview!

Santa, in a room full of people:

"I need space. I'm Claus-trophobic!"

Why did the ornament go to the party?

To "hang out"!

Why did the Grinch browse the web?

To download joy!

What do snowmen do on Christmas?

Play freeze tag!

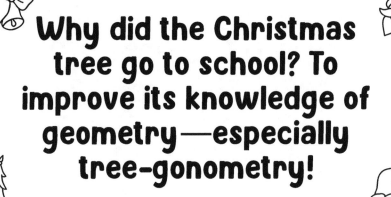

Why did the Christmas tree go to school? To improve its knowledge of geometry—especially tree-gonometry!

The Snowman told his son, "You melt my heart!"

Why was the snowman browsing books?

Because he was looking for some "chilling" tales!

How do you compliment Santa's garden?

"Mistletoe-tally awesome!"

Why did the Snowman call tech support?

His "frost" drive was broken!

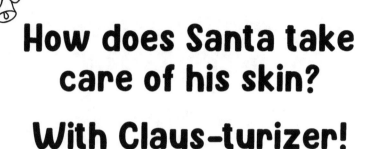

How does Santa take care of his skin?

With Claus-turizer!

Why did the cookie visit the doctor?

Because he felt crumby during Christmas!

Why did Rudolph become an astronaut?

To guide the spaceship tonight!

Why did the scarecrow get a bonus during Christmas?

Because of his outstanding performance in the field!

How does Darth Vader celebrate Christmas?

By feeling the festive side of the Force!

Why did the Christmas tree need help?

It had a breakdown and lost its tinsel!

Why did the elf take up meditation?

To find his inner elf!

Why did the Snowman see a counselor?

His emotions kept melting!

How did the gingerbread man comfort his friend?

"Don't crumble under pressure; we've got this!"

Why did the Snowman want a promotion?

He wanted to be an "ice-ecutive"!

What do you call an old snowman?

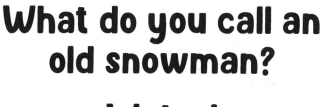

Water!

Why did the reindeer wear a bell?

He wanted to jingle all the way!

Why did the gingerbread man sunbathe?

To get a crispy tan!

Why was Santa always calm?

He knew how to "sleigh" his stress!

What's an elf's favorite type of picture?

Elf-ies!

How did the Snowman fall ill?

He caught a "frostbite"!

The Snowman at a diner: "I'll have the frosty fries with a side of freeze, please!"

What kind of car does Santa drive in the off-season?

A Claus-tang!

Why did the Christmas tree feel bad?

It had tinsel-itis!

What did the Snowman say about the windy weather?

"It blows my mind!"

Why did the gingerbread man attend the spa?

He needed to be kneaded!

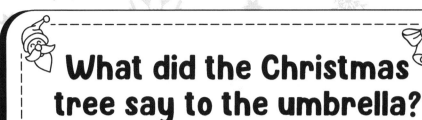

What did the Christmas tree say to the umbrella?

"You're all branch and no leaves!"

Why did Santa join the band?

He wanted to play the Claus-tanets!

How does a snowman secure his scarf?

With an ice clip!

What's Santa's dog's name?

Santa Paws!

How did the elf get to the top floor?

By the "elf"-evator!

What did Santa say to the Snowman?

"Stay frosty!"

How does Santa take care of his beard?

With Claus-ditioner!

How did the ornament react to the joke?

It cracked up!

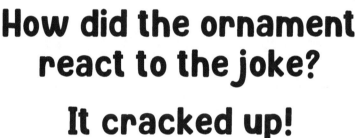

Why did the Snowman visit the therapist?

He felt he had too many "layers" to unpack!

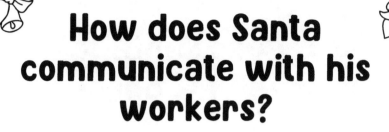

How does Santa communicate with his workers?

Through "elf"-mail!

Why did Santa become a detective?

To find out who was naughty or nice!

How does Santa's cat greet him?

"Purr-y Christmas!"

Why was the Snowman always zen?

He had an icy, calm demeanor!

What do you call a fit snowman?

An abs-olutely cool dude!

Why did the elf apply for a construction job?

He heard they needed a little help with the building!

How does a snowman get fit?

By doing "ice-sometrics"!

Why did the reindeer study the weather?

He wanted to know when it would "rein"!

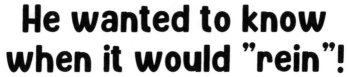

What do you call a cat in the Arctic?

Purr-sicle!

Snowman at the beach:

"I'm here to chill out and melt down!"

Santa's day off?

Binging on North Pole-flix!

Why did the Christmas tree get glasses?

To spruce up its look!

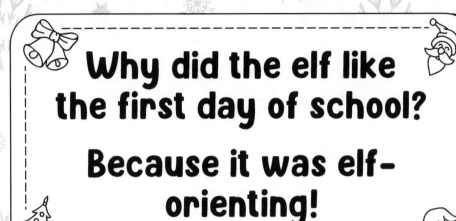

Why did the elf like the first day of school?

Because it was elf-orienting!

Snowman's cereal choice?

Snowy O's!

What is the snow couple's favorite communication tool?

Snow-mojis!

How does a snowman stay fit?

Ice aerobics!

What do you call Santa's helpers who take care of his suit?

Claus-tumiers!

Why did the Snowman bring a notebook to the party?

He wanted to "break the ice" with cool stories!

Why did Santa become a chef?

Because he loves to "whisk" it!

Why did the reindeer wear glasses?

To sleigh the reading game!

Snowman's breakfast?

Frosted doughnuts!

How did Santa rate his sleigh on the App Store?

Five stars for fast delivery!

How did the reindeer know he was good at baseball?

He was a star pitcher in the reindeer games!

Why did Santa's sleigh never fail?

It was always uplifted by festive spirit!

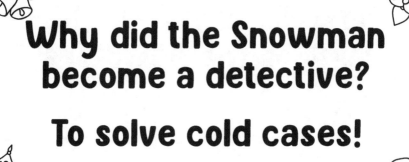

Why did the Snowman become a detective?

To solve cold cases!

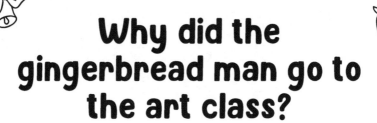

Why did the gingerbread man go to the art class?

To learn cookie painting!

Why did the Christmas tree join a dance class?

To shake its baubles!

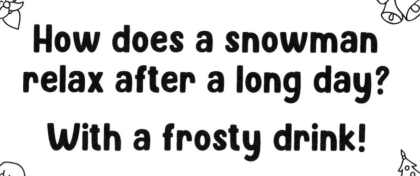

How does a snowman relax after a long day?

With a frosty drink!

Why was the Snowman always happy?

Because he had a heart of snow!

Why did the elf take up gardening?

He wanted to grow his elf-esteem!

Snowman's baby name?

Mini-melt!

How do reindeer celebrate a job well done?

With a high hoof!

Why did the gingerbread man go on a diet?

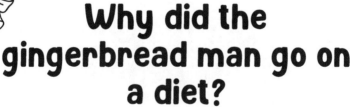

Too many sweet encounters!

Why did Santa use an umbrella?

To shield himself from the "rein"!

How does a snowman get around town?

On his snowmobile!

What do you call a Christmas tree with a lot of dollar bills?

A tree-mendous fortune!

Why did the reindeer become a journalist?

He wanted to get the scoop on Santa!

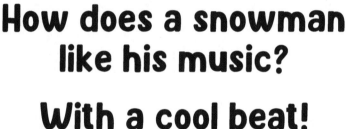

How does a snowman like his music?

With a cool beat!

Why was the Snowman a great musician?

He has built-in drumsticks!

What's a snowman's favorite vegetable?

A carrot, but only for his nose!

Why did the Christmas tree feel popular?

Because it was always surrounded by presents!

Why did Santa become a baker?

He kneaded a change!

Why did the Snowman visit the tropical island?

He wanted to thaw out a little!

What's a snowman's favorite type of math?

Snow-metry!

Why did the reindeer wear sunglasses?

Because his future was so bright!

What did the Snowman name his dog?

Frostbite!

What's Santa's favorite candy?

Holly Jollies!

Why did the Snowman go to the dentist?

To get his "frost-bite" checked!

What kind of photos does Santa take?

Elf-portraits!

What did the Snowman say to his therapist?

"I have melting anxiety!"

How did the Christmas tree light up the room?

With its dazzling personality!

Why did the elf apply to law school?

To understand Santa's Claus-es!

Why did the Snowman visit the tailor?

He felt his buttons were loose!

What do you call Santa when he loses his pants?

Saint Knickerless!

Why did the elf refuse to play cards?

He wanted to "deck" the halls!

Why did the Snowman visit the music store?

He wanted cool tunes!

How did the Christmas tree feel after a haircut?

Truncated!

Why did the Snowman drink cold coffee?

He didn't want to risk a meltdown!

Why was the elf good at math?

He mastered "add-elf-tion"!

What did Santa say to the stressed worker?

"Yule be okay!"

Why did the gingerbread man avoid the river?

Because he didn't want to become a soggy cookie!

Why did the Snowman decline the invitation to the sauna?

Too steamy for his liking!

How did the reindeer describe the fancy party?

"Deer-lightful"!

Why did the Christmas tree get a computer?

To log in!

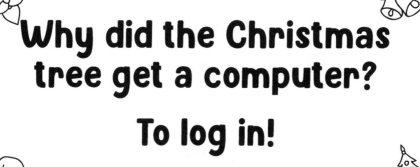

How does a snowman stay safe online?

He avoids the meltware!

Why was the gingerbread man a great detective?

He always followed the crumbs!

How do snowmen stay in shape?

They have "ice-robics" sessions!

Why did the elf refuse to share his toy?

It was elf-made!

Why did the reindeer attend dance classes?

To master the "rein"-dance!

Why did the Christmas tree go to therapy?

It had tangled thoughts!

How does the Snowman fight off enemies?

With snowballs!

Why did the gingerbread man see a therapist?

He felt his life was crumbling!

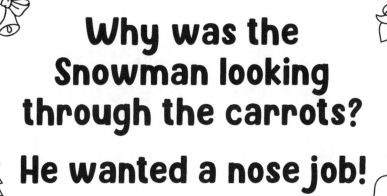

Why was the Snowman looking through the carrots?

He wanted a nose job!

What did the reindeer say to the cold elf?

"Come stand by me; I've got a built-in "fur" nace!"

Why did the Christmas tree seek adventure?

It wanted to branch out!

How does Santa respond to haters?

"Ho-Ho-Hope you find some joy!"

Why did the Snowman bring a sunhat?

He wanted to play it cool!

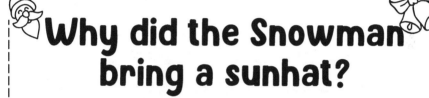

Why did Santa bring a broom?

To sweep away the Grinch's negativity!

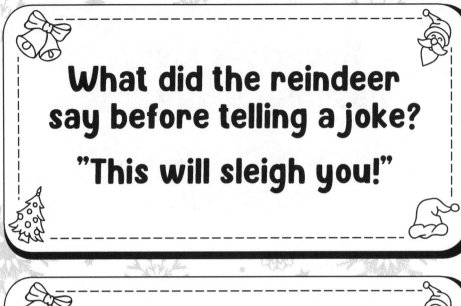

What did the reindeer say before telling a joke?

"This will sleigh you!"

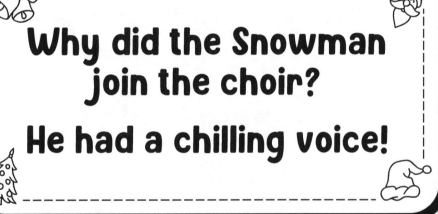

Why did the Snowman join the choir?

He had a chilling voice!

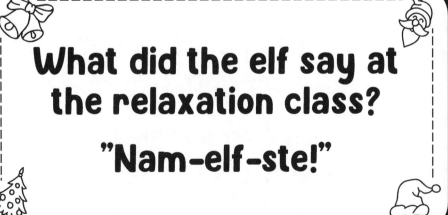

What did the elf say at the relaxation class?

"Nam-elf-ste!"

Why did the gingerbread man need insurance?

To protect himself from crumbling assets!

How does a snowman show his disapproval?

"That's snow good!"

Why was the elf always confident?

He believed in "elf-care"!

How do you call a reindeer with three eyes?

Reiiindeer!

Why did the Snowman become a referee?

He believed in fair play and cold judgment!

What's a snowman's favorite salad?

Iceberg lettuce!

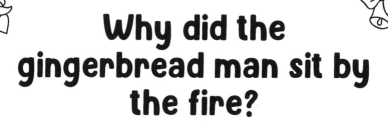

Why did the gingerbread man sit by the fire?

He wanted to be toasted!

How did the Snowman describe his vacation?

"Ice-caped to paradise!"

How does a Christmas tree feel after a big meal?

Pine and dandy!

Why did the reindeer eat the Christmas decorations?

He wanted to have a festive feeling inside!

How do elves express themselves online?

Using "elf-mojis"!

What did the Snowman say to the impatient ice cube?

"Chill out!"

Why did the elf carry a notebook?

To jot down "elf-observations"!

What did the Christmas tree ask for at the salon?

A festive trim!

What accessory does a reindeer wear to the party?

A "deerlightful" tiara!

How does Santa organize his elves?

In elf-abetical order!

Why was the Snowman feeling blue?

He had a frosty reception!

Why did the elf love the computer?

He was great at typing on the keyboard elf-abet!

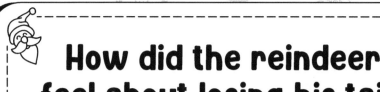

How did the reindeer feel about losing his tail?

He said, "It's behind me now!"

Why did Santa get a new sleigh?

The old one needed Claus-tly repairs!

How did the gingerbread man keep his hair in place?

With cookie gel!

Why did the elf put his bed in the fireplace?

He wanted to sleep like a log!

How do snowmen communicate?

Through their icy stares!

Why was the reindeer's report card so impressive?

It had all D's for 'deer-lightful'!

Why was the Snowman always smiling?

He knew that no two flakes were alike!

Why did the elf refuse to play the piano?

He was scared of the sharp notes!

How does Santa react when his sleigh breaks down?

"It's sleigh-tly annoying!"

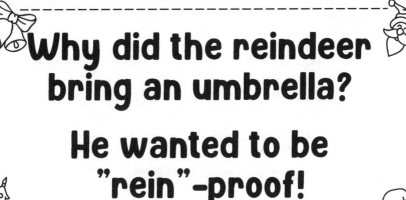

Why did the reindeer bring an umbrella?

He wanted to be "rein"-proof!

Why did the Christmas tree go to therapy?

It felt wooden inside!

What did the snowman order at the restaurant?

A bowl of chili!

What did the Snowman do when he was upset?

He gave everyone the cold shoulder!

How did the reindeer describe his tough day?

"It was deer-pressing!"

Why did the Christmas tree always get in trouble?

It was knotty by nature!

What did the Snowman say to the winter wind?

"Blow me away!"

Why was the gingerbread man always brave?

He didn't crumble under pressure!

How does Santa stay fit?

He does Claus-thenics!

Why did the elf sit on the clock?

He wanted to be on time!

What's a snowman's favorite dance?

The icy shuffle!

Why did the reindeer join the theater?

He was great at "stag" - ing performances!

Why was the Snowman always calm?

He had a lot of cool thoughts!

Why did Santa start using the elevator?

To give his reindeer a break!

What's a reindeer's favorite type of movie?

Anything that's deer-lightful!

Why did the Snowman go to school?

To become a little snow-it-all!

Why did the gingerbread man visit the hospital?

Because he had a few cookie crumbles!

What do you call a reindeer who tells secrets?

Rudolf the Red-nosed Gossiper!

How does a snowman laugh?

With a chilling "he-he-he"!

How does a gingerbread man surf the web?

By using cookies!

What did the Snowman say about the blizzard?

"It's an avalanche of fun!"

What did the Snowman call his son?

"A chip off the old block of ice!"

Why was the gingerbread man a smart investor?

He knew where to put his dough!

Why did the gingerbread man see a dentist?

He had sweet tooth issues!

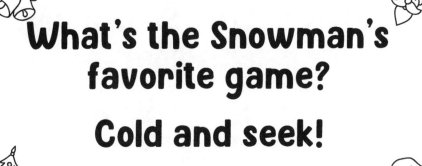

What's the Snowman's favorite game?

Cold and seek!

Why did the elf bring a ladder to the bar?

He heard that the drinks were on the house!

Why did the elf apply for a job in the library?

He loved elf-published books!

Why did the Christmas tree get a computer?

To spruce up its web presence!

How did the Snowman know it was going to be a frosty day?

He read the weather "flake-cast"!

Why was the gingerbread man great at baseball?

He was a perfect batter!

What's Santa's favorite type of music?

Wrap!

How does a reindeer ask for dessert?

"Can I have another piece of pie, deer?"

What do gingerbread men use to fix their houses?

Icing and gumdrop nails!

Why did the Snowman decline the theater invitation?

He feared he'd melt under the spotlight!

How does Santa get into houses without chimneys?

Through the "elf"-evator!

How does Santa invest his money?

In the "stocking" market!

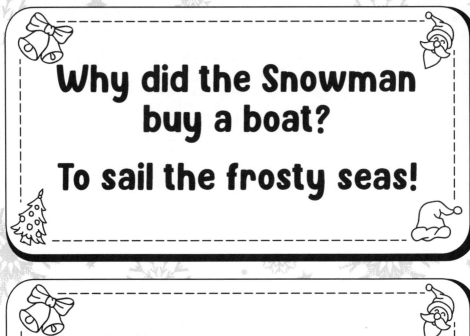

Why did the Snowman buy a boat?

To sail the frosty seas!

What did the rapper elf name his newborn?

Lil' Jingle!

What's a Christmas tree's go-to candy?

Piner-mints!

How does a reindeer greet his friends?

"Merry Christ-moose!"

Why did the gingerbread man join the police?

He had a knack for crumb-solving!

Why did Santa start gardening?

He wanted to grow his presents!

Why was the gingerbread man good at school?

He was one smart cookie!

How does Santa capture moments?

With his North Polaroid!

What do elves send out during Christmas?

Elf-agrams!

How does a snowman avoid rush hour?

By taking the glacier express!

What do you get if you mix Santa with a lawyer?

Santa Sues, defending the North Pole's rights!

How do snowmen make new friends?

They have ice-breakers!

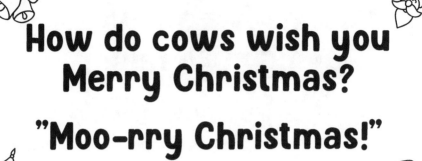

How do cows wish you Merry Christmas?

"Moo-rry Christmas!"

What's red, green, and sometimes blue?

A Christmas light left out in the cold!

What did the snowflake say to the gingerbread man?

"Chill out, cookie!"

How would you describe a frozen elf in a song?

"Jingle Brrr"!

How did the turkey share the festive spirit?

By gobbling up the love!

Elf's new post on social media:

"Life's short; spread the sparkle!"

How do snowmen compliment each other?

"You're snow cool!"

Why is Santa's factory eco-friendly?

It's elf-sustained!

Why did the elf bring a magnifying glass?

To zoom in on the holiday cheer!

What's the gingerbread man's favorite song?

"Cookie Cutter Blues"!

What did the tree branch say to the tree ornament?

"Hang in there!"

How does a Christmas tree get internet?

It connects to the tree-Fi hotspot!

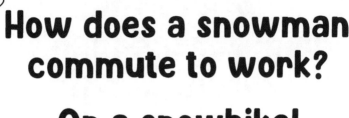

How does a snowman commute to work?

On a snowbike!

My spouse mentioned she would incinerate my Christmas gift if it wasn't to her taste. Hence, I chose a candle.

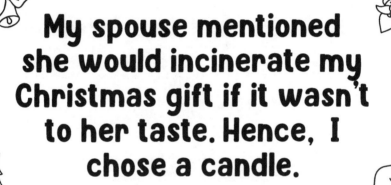

Why was the advent calendar feeling stressed?

Because its days were numbered!

Why don't snowmen ever have secrets?

Because they tend to blabber snow much!

Why did the snowflake break up with the Snowman?

Because he had too much frosty attitude!

What did the grape say to the raisin at Christmas dinner? "Looks like you've had too much Christmas spirit!"

Why was the Christmas tree always in trouble?

Because it was always pining for attention!

What do you get when you cross an apple with a Christmas tree?

A pineapple!

Why was the Snowman always stressed?

Because he couldn't keep his cool!

What did the snowflake say to the other snowflake?

"I think we have a flakey relationship!"

What did the Christmas tree say to the lumberjack?

"Leaf me alone!"

What do you call a snowman that became a detective?

Sherlock Cold!

Made in the USA
Columbia, SC
01 December 2023

27552131R00061